JOE BIDEN

by Jaclyn Jaycox

PEBBLE
a capstone imprint

Published by Pebble, an imprint of Capstone
1710 Roe Crest Drive, North Mankato, Minnesota 56003
capstonepub.com

Library of Congress Cataloging-in-Publication Data
Names: Jaycox, Jaclyn, 1983- author.
Title: Joe Biden / by Jaclyn Jaycox.
Description: North Mankato, Minnesota : Published by Pebble, an imprint of Capstone, [2023] | Series: Biographies | Includes bibliographical references and index. | Audience: Ages 5-8 | Audience: Grades K-1 | Summary: "How much do you know about President Joe Biden? Find out the facts you need to know about the 46th president of the United States. You'll learn about Joe's early life, challenges he overcame, and the accomplishments of this American leader"— Provided by publisher.
Identifiers: LCCN 2021061410 (print) | LCCN 2021061411 (ebook) | ISBN 9781666350548 (hardcover) | ISBN 9781666350739 (paperback) | ISBN 9781666350692 (pdf) | ISBN 9781666350616 (kindle edition)
Subjects: LCSH: Biden, Joseph R., Jr.—Juvenile literature. | United States—Politics and government—1989—-Juvenile literature. | Presidents—United States—Biography—Juvenile literature. | Politicians—United States—Biography—Juvenile literature. | Legislators—United States—Biography—Juvenile literature. | United States—Politics and government—1945-1989—Juvenile literature. | Delaware—Biography—Juvenile literature.
Classification: LCC E917 .J39 2023 (print) | LCC E917 (ebook) | DDC 973.934092 [B]—dc23
LC record available at https://lccn.loc.gov/2021061410
LC ebook record available at https://lccn.loc.gov/2021061411

Editorial Credits
Editor: Mandy Robbins; Designer: Hilary Wacholz; Media Researcher: Jo Miller; Production Specialist: Tori Abraham

Image Credits
Alamy: ARCHIVIO GBB, 7, Geopix, 5, REUTERS, 25; Associated Press: AP Photo, 13, Enric Marti, 21, File, 14; Executive Office of the President of the United States/Adam Schultz, Cover, 1; Getty Images: Alex Potemkin, 6, Bettmann, 11, Cynthia Johnson, 15, Denis Jr. Tangney, 9; Shutterstock: Andrew Cline, 27, BiksuTong, 26, Everett Collection, 23, mark reinstein, 17, 19, Naresh111, 29

Table of Contents

Words in **bold** are in the glossary.

Who Is Joe Biden?

Joe Biden is the 46th president of the United States. He started in **politics** when he was 27 years old. Joe wanted to help people. He wanted to make their lives better.

Joe has made history. He was one of the youngest U.S. **senators**. He was Delaware's longest-serving senator. In 2021, he became the oldest president in history.

Growing Up Joe

Joseph Biden Jr. was born November 20, 1942. He grew up in Scranton, Pennsylvania. He was the oldest of four children. When he was 10 years old, his family moved to Claymont, Delaware. His mom was a homemaker. His dad was a car salesman.

Scranton, Pennsylvania

Joe Biden, age 9

Joe **stuttered** growing up. Kids at school bullied him. He worked hard to stop. He read poetry aloud while looking in the mirror. Slowly, his speech got better.

In high school, Joe played football. He was good. His classmates stopped teasing him. Joe graduated in 1961.

Joe went on to the University of Delaware. He became interested in politics. He studied political science and history. After college, Joe went to law school. He went to Syracuse University in New York.

Syracuse University

Starting a Family and Career

In college, Joe met Neilia Hunter. They married in 1966. They had three children. Their names were Beau, Hunter, and Naomi.

Joe finished law school in 1968. He became a lawyer in Delaware. But he was still interested in politics. Joe ran for New Castle County Council. He was **elected** in 1970. He continued practicing law. He even started his own law firm.

Joe, his wife, Neilia, and their two sons on Joe's 30th birthday

In 1972, Joe ran for the U.S. **Senate**. He was only 29. Joe became one of the youngest people ever elected. But he almost quit before he started.

In December 1972, Joe's family was in a car accident. Neilia and Naomi were killed. Hunter and Beau were badly hurt. Joe was heartbroken. He wanted to give up his seat in the Senate. He wanted to stay with his sons. Family members talked him out of it.

Joe stands by his wife, Neilia, and holds his sons at a political event in 1972.

On January 5, 1973, Joe was sworn into office. It happened from his sons' hospital room.

Joe stayed living in Wilmington, Delaware. He traveled to and from Washington, D.C., every day. It was about 120 miles (195 kilometers) each way. But he came home every night.

Joe married Jill Jacobs in 1977. She was a teacher. Together they had a daughter, Ashley.

Senator Biden

Joe spent 36 years in the Senate. He was reelected six times. No other Delaware senator has stayed in office that long. Joe helped write many **bills.**

In 1986, Joe wrote one of the first **climate change** bills. He wanted to learn more about climate change. He wanted the government to create ideas to fight it. The bill became a law the next year.

Joe has been part of special **committees**. One was made up of 22 senators. It oversaw the Department of Justice. This department made sure laws were followed.

On this committee, Joe helped write another bill. It is the Violence Against Women Act. It asked for tougher sentences for people who hurt women. It also gave help to survivors. The act was passed in 1994. Crimes against women went down.

Joe (far right) serves on the Senate Judiciary Committee in 1987.

Joe was also on another important committee. It focused on the United States' relationship with other countries. It decided when to help other countries.

The committee also made decisions to keep the United States safe from enemies. Joe traveled all around the world. He met many world leaders. He was the head of this committee for many years. Joe was very respected in this area of politics.

Joe jokes with children in Afghanistan in 2002.

Road to the Presidency

In 2008, Joe ran for president. He later dropped out. But it didn't end there. Barack Obama was in the running. He asked Joe to run with him as vice president. Joe accepted. They won. In January 2009, Joe became the 47th vice president. He served eight years in this role.

Joe also suffered more loss. His son Beau learned he had brain cancer in 2013. Two years later, Beau died.

The Obamas and the Bidens celebrate their 2008 win.

Joe did not run for president in 2016. He helped fight cancer instead. Joe and his wife started a program. They brought cancer **researchers** together. They want to find a cure.

In 2017, Joe was awarded the Presidential Medal of Freedom. It is the highest honor a person can get. He got it for years of service to Americans.

In 2020, Joe ran for president again. This time, he won. He chose Kamala Harris as his vice president. She is the first person with Black and Indian American parents to become vice president. She is the first woman vice president too.

Kamala Harris

On January 20, 2021, Joe was sworn in as president of the United States. He cares about people. In his speech, he promised to work to **unite** people.

Important Dates

November 20, 1942 — Joseph Biden Jr. is born in Scranton, Pennsylvania.

1961 — Joe enters the University of Delaware.

1966 — Joe marries Neilia Hunter.

1970 — Joe is elected to the New Castle County Council in Delaware.

December 1972 — Joe's wife and daughter, Naomi, are killed in a car accident.

January 5, 1973 — Joe is sworn into office as a U.S. senator.

1977 — Joe marries Jill Jacobs.

1986 — Joe writes one of the first climate change bills.

1994 — Joe's bill, the Violence Against Women Act, is passed into law.

January 2009 — Joe is sworn into office as the vice president of the United States.

2015 — Joe's son Beau dies of brain cancer.

2017 — Joe receives the Presidential Medal of Freedom.

January 20, 2021 — Joe is sworn in as president of the United States.

Fast Facts

Name:
Joseph Biden Jr.

Role:
46th president of the United States

Life dates:
November 20, 1942, to present

Key accomplishments:
Joe has spent much of his life in politics. He has been a U.S. senator, vice president, and president. He has worked to make the world a better, safer place.

Glossary

bill (BIL)—a written idea for a new law

climate change (KLY-muht CHAYNJ)—a significant change in Earth's climate over a period of time

committee (kuh-MI-tee)—a group of people chosen to discuss things and make decisions for a larger group

elect (i-LEKT)—to choose someone as a leader by voting

politics (POL-uh-tiks)—the debate and activity involved in governing a country

researcher (REE-surch-ur)—someone who studies a subject to discover new information

Senate (SEN–it)—one of the two houses of Congress that makes laws

senator (SEN-ah-tur)—one of the 100 people in the Senate who make laws

stutter (STUH-tuhr)—a speech problem that causes a person to repeat the first sound of a word

unite (YOO-nite)—to join together

Read More

Hansen, Grace. *Joe Biden*. Minneapolis: Abdo Kids, 2021.

Monroe, Alex. *Joe Biden*. Minneapolis: Bellwether Media, Inc., 2022.

Rustad, Martha E.H. *The President of the United States*. North Mankato, MN: Pebble, 2020.

Internet Sites

Biography of President Joe Biden
ducksters.com/biography/uspresidents/josephbiden.
php

Joe Biden
americanhistoryforkids.com/joe-biden/

Joe Biden
kids.nationalgeographic.com/history/article/joe-biden

Index

About the Author

Jaclyn Jaycox is a children's book author and editor. When she's not writing, she loves reading and spending time with her family. She lives in southern Minnesota with her husband, two kids, and a spunky goldendoodle.